This Book Belongs To:

____

____

____

Abundance is my Birthright.

Generational
wealth
begins with
me

Be open
to all
opportunities

Gratitude
is
always
the right
attitude.

Run your
own race
and
win it.

Always be confident.

Always
be
optimistic
and see
the
good

I am
worthy of
unlimited
blessings.

In everything, I am enough

Always
be
grateful
for your
blessings

Identify your gift and use it often

You are
uniquely
valuable

Protect
your
self-esteem

Abundance is already yours. Go claim it.

Start
where you are
with
what you have

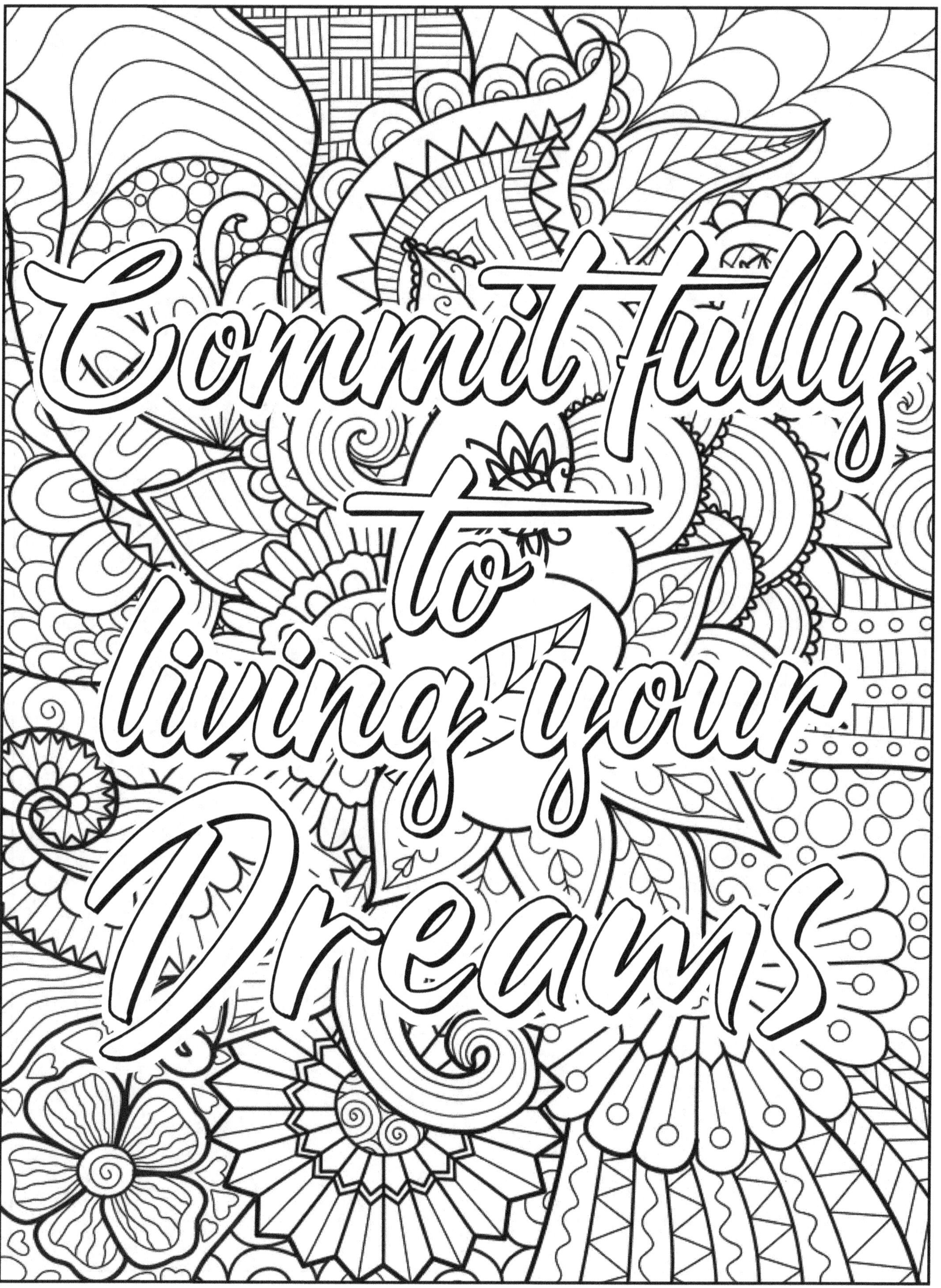

Commit fully
to
living your
Dreams

Accept no
Limitations.

Use
intangible
assets
to create
tangible
benefits...

Be excellent in everything that you do.

OWN YOUR
GREATNESS
WITH
CONFIDENCE.

Health
is your
wealth
Protect it

YOU ARE
LIMITLESS
AND
TALENTED

Embrace your fear.
Do it anyway.

Make people
feel appreciated.

Invest in yourself often & early.

Be honest in all circumstances.

Poverty feeds on the wrong mindset.

Always
be your
authentic
self.

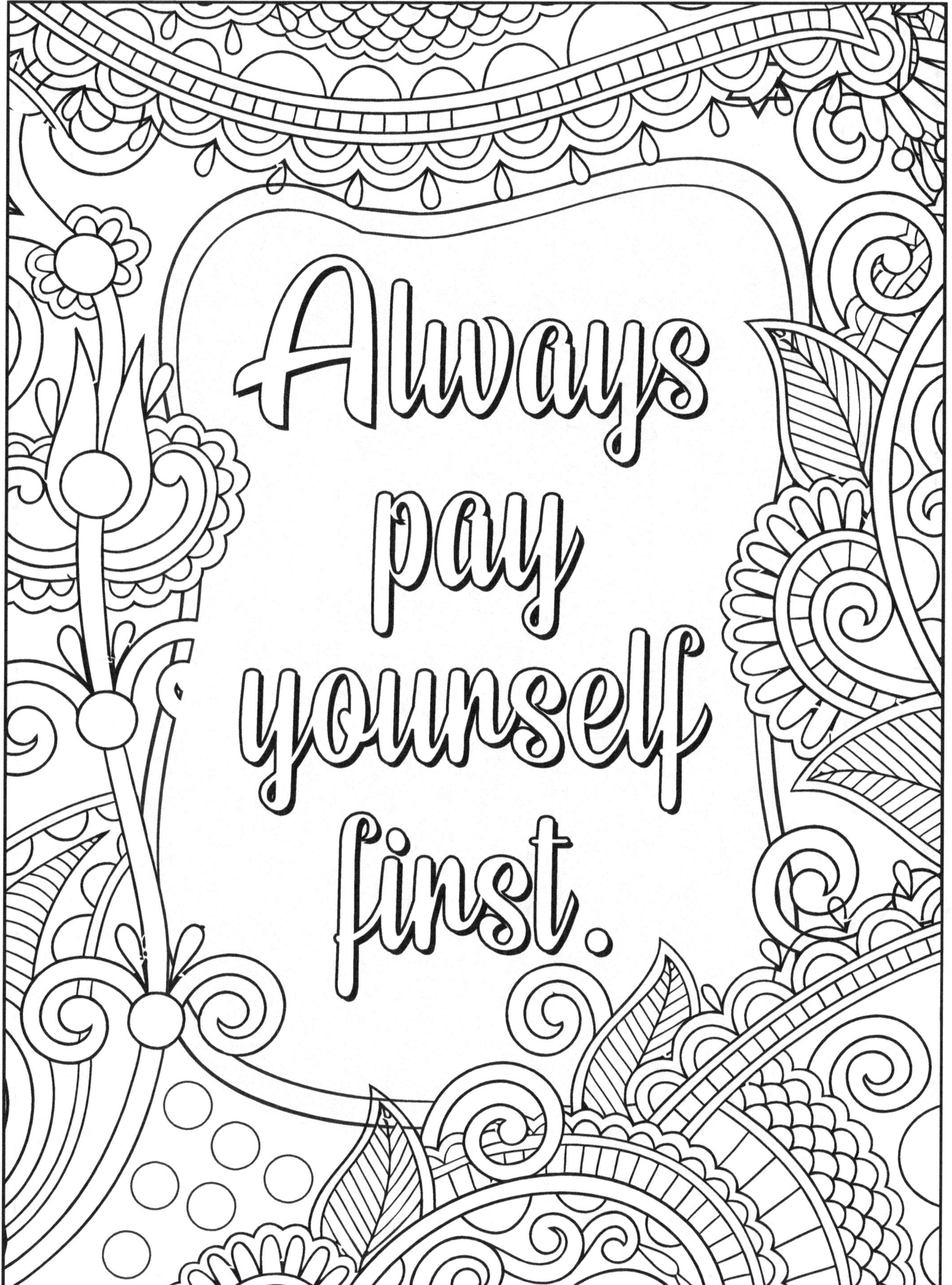

Always
pay
yourself
first.

YOU ARE
EXACTLY
WHAT YOU
THINK YOU ARE.

Remain open
to learning
new things

Ask for
what you
want
boldly.

Find a mentor
that's living
the life
that you want.

Understand
the rule of
72.

Start saving while you're young.

Learn how the stock market works.

Tomorrow doesn't exist. Do it today.

A positive attitude will take you far.

Always
choose faith
over fear

Always pay
what you owe

Obstacles are created by your mind

Love
yourself
unconditionally

Take
responsibility
for your
actions

Always put your well-being first.

Always
keep your
word

Only put your money where it will grow.

Use
life insurance
to build
wealth

Success
and
struggle
are both
a
choice

Leverage the time value of money

Believe
in yourself.
You can
do anything.

9 780578 985497